ISSN

Dediu Newsletter

Author: Michael M. Dediu

Monthly news, reviews, comments and suggestions for a better and wiser world

---

Vol. 3, Nr. 5 (29), 6 April 2019

DERC Publishing House

Tewksbury (Boston), Massachusetts, U. S. A.

For subscriptions please use the contact form at www.derc.com

Published and printed in the
United States of America
On the Great Seal of the United States are included:
E Pluribus Unum (Out of many, one)
Annuit Coeptis (He has approved of the undertakings)
Novus Ordo Seclorum (New order of the ages)

Dediu, Michael M.

Dediu Newsletter Vol 3, Number 5 (29), 6 April 2019
Monthly reviews, comments and suggestions for a better and
wiser world

ISSN 2475-2061
ISBN 978-1-939757-87-6

Preface

March 2019, with its famous π day on the 14th, and the splendid March Equinox on the 20th (completely unrelated to the start of the spring, which can be – depending on the location in the northern hemisphere - between the end of February and the beginning of April), brought us all kinds of news: on March 4th astronauts have entered SpaceX's Crew Dragon while in orbit for the first time, just hours after the commercial spacecraft docked at the International Space Station; the U.S. debt grows by about $2 B/day, now is over $22.1 T; specialists created a new method that could rapidly detect cancer in cells; Jeff Bezos hosted his annual Mars Conference in Palm Springs, California; new battery research may result in high-performance batteries made entirely from polymeric materials; machine learning, AI and other exponentially growing technologies (all based on mathematics) are transforming businesses, the political economy, and our society on this planet..

In this 5th newsletter of the third volume, the 29th in total, we included the most relevant news, in a balanced approach, usually directly from the source, to help the general public better understand the realities around us. We included also several nice photos - I thank my wife for her photo assistance. Being well and correctly informed is a sine qua non requirement for everybody, in order to make the right decisions for the future.

Enjoy this newsletter and be optimist!

Michael M. Dediu, Ph. D.

Tewksbury (Boston), U. S. A., 6 April 2019

Paris: Musée du Louvre (1793): a statue representing art, in front of Pavillion Richelieu. in Cour Napoléon (1803). The museum is housed in the Palais du Louvre, originally built as a fortress around 1190 under Philip II of France (1165 – 1223, king 1179 – 1223).

Table of Contents

Table of Contents

Preface 3

Table of Contents 5

United States of America 7

China, Japan, and neighbors 13

Russia, Switzerland, Eastern Europe 21

United Kingdom, Canada, South America............................ 25

France, Germany, and neighbors 28

India, Pakistan, Australia, and neighbors............................ 36

Italy, Middle East, Africa 39

Medical 49

Mathematics, Science & Artificial Intelligence (AI) 56

General news and issues 59

Humor... 62

Universe Axioms 63

Time Axioms... 65

Bibliography 66

Japan, Tsukuba, 20 Nov 2008, inside the main research building, photographs with celebrity physicists, like Isaac Newton (right down), Galileo Galilei (1564 – 1642, who used the Leaning Tower of Pisa, Italy (1173 – 1372), center-right), at the High Energy Accelerator Research Organization (KEK, 1997) in Tsukuba Science City (1962), in Ibaraki Prefecture, 60 km north-east of Tokyo.

United States of America

(Population 324.4 M, rank 3, growth 0.7%. Free: 89 of 100. Area 9.52 M km^2, rank 4.).

4 March 2019. Reports. Astronauts have entered SpaceX's Crew Dragon while in orbit for the first time, just hours after the commercial spacecraft docked at the International Space Station. The voyage also marks the first time since 2011, when NASA retired its space shuttle fleet, that a spacecraft designed and built in the U.S. to carry people, has been blasted into orbit.

Reports: Many people are asking: is Uncle Sam going to take out of private hands millions more acres of America's valuable land mass? This is the reverse of privatization — it is the nationalizing of our nation's farm land, forests, streams and pastures.

Reports: The number of Americans without access to high-speed Internet dropped in the last 10 years by 56% – from 78.9 millions to 34.8 millions.

Reports: Recent data from the Fed indicated that credit card debt is rising faster than mortgage debt, student loan balances and auto debt. Credit card debt at the end of December topped $870 B and re-touched the "nominal peak" level of 2008.

Reports: Cybercriminals use technical scams, especially targeting senior citizens. The DOJ wants to crack down on scams including cybercriminals posing as workers from the tech companies. The cybercriminals convince targets to provide remote access to computers, which can be used to drain bank accounts or access sensitive information.

People ask the authorities, for many years, to arrest the cybercriminals.

Reports: Economists are still frustrated by the lack of data and delays prompted by the government shutdown.

Reports: The median age is 46 for the 59 Democrats who assumed office this year. Sixteen of these members are under 39. Nancy Pelosi is 79. The average age of the Democratic leadership is 71.

Reports: As usual, Federal agencies billed taxpayers millions for lobster tail, alcohol, standing desks, golf carts, and more frivolous expenditures, before budgets ran out at the end of the fiscal year. A new analysis released by OpenTheBooks.com found 66 agencies spent $97 B last September, the final month of fiscal year 2018. The end of the year taxpayer-funded spending spree included contracts with Coors, millions on iPhones, furniture, and CrossFit equipment. "In the final month of the fiscal year, federal agencies scramble to spend what's left in their annual budget," OpenTheBooks.com said. "Agencies worry spending less than their budget allows might prompt Congress to appropriate less money in the next fiscal year. To avoid this, federal agencies choose to embark on an annual shopping spree rather than admit they can operate on less." Resulting government expenditures included $4.6 M on lobster tail and crab; $673,471 on golf carts; $1.7 million on pianos, tubas, and trombones; $9.8 M on workout and recreation equipment; and $7.7 M iPhones and iPads.

Reports: All wealth is initially created in the private sector, and government spending is the wasteful consequence. We know it's wasteful because we know that bad ideas in government almost never die. A front-page Wall Street Journal article from Tuesday, 5 March, shows that even though airplanes can transport passengers from Chicago to St. Louis in less than 1 hour, Amtrak (our national train service) has a train route in place that can similarly transport passengers between the two cities. The problem is that what takes less than an hour by plane takes 5.5 hours by train. Sadly, the Amtrak story gets worse.

Reports: Deficits are covered with money printing, which is not good. - U.S. personal income falls; spending weakest since 2009. - Politicians will talk about anything, but our ballooning national debt. - While the Beltway class hyperventilates about the buzz du jour, there's one subject all of them studiously avoid: our $22.1 T. -

Our debt grows by about $2 billion a day. The U.S. has maintained a federal debt since Herbert Hoover was in office, and it keeps growing. Today, the debt jumps by another million dollars every 41 seconds, or about $2 billions a day. Since it's an awkward topic, politicians focus on anything else, usually involving more spending. While lawmakers debate free college, free health care and a big, beautiful wall, the debt clock keeps on spinning. -According to the most recent figures, our debt is 4% higher than our gross domestic product. - U.S. credit card debt closed 2018 at a record $870 B. - For all the worries about middle-aged men, it is actually men at the younger end of the prime-age years who have seen the sharpest drop in employment rates: - Political studies became irrelevant. - Connecticut parents are challenging racial quotas in our kids' schools.

12 March 2019. Reports: ATLANTIC Ocean - NASA passed a major milestone this morning, in its goal to restore America's human spaceflight capability, when SpaceX's Crew Dragon returned to Earth after a five-day mission docked to the International Space Station. About 6 hours after departing the space station, Crew Dragon splashed down at 8:45 a.m. EST approximately 370 km (230 miles) off the coast of Cape Canaveral, Florida. SpaceX retrieved the spacecraft from the Atlantic Ocean, and is transporting it back to port on the company's recovery ship.

12 March 2019. Reports: The White House proposed a $4.7 T fiscal 2020 budget on Monday, 11 March, that called for cutting regular non-defense discretionary spending by 9%, while increasing defense spending by 4.7%, and including $8.6 B for a border wall. The White House is asking Congress for $718.3 B in federal fiscal year 2020, which represents a 4.7% increase over this year's military budget, according to budget figures, which would represent another record year for U.S. defense spending. Under the blueprint, the budget doesn't balance in 10 years, and shows a $202 B deficit in 2029, assuming economic growth at an average of 3% for the decade. The proposal is likely to be dismissed by Congress, and increases the threat of another government shutdown in the fall.

12 March 2019. Reports: Retailers - including Dollar Tree, Abercrombie & Fitch, Kohl's, Gap, J.C. Penney, and Tesla - have already announced 4,810 store closures in 2019. According to Coresight Research, the closings far outweigh the openings. Last year, Coresight tracked 5,524 store shutterings, down more than 30% from a record 8,139 closures announced in 2017.

12 March 2019. Reports: America only works when its people work. The welfare reforms are needed: we have a crisis of folks not working in this country. Despite record-low unemployment, millions are missing out on the benefits – both financial and otherwise – of work. The labor force participation rate still sits at just 63% – three points lower than at the start of the Great Recession in 2008. And nowhere is this economic paradox more apparent than in the welfare system, where millions of able-bodied adults have been sitting on the sidelines.

Reports: Many educators say that the U.S. have a national reading crisis.

Reports: Rep. Andy Biggs (R-AZ) mentioned that the most basic purpose of the federal government is to protect Americans from enemies, foreign and domestic. A few days ago, our national debt surpassed $22 T. Since 2017, the national debt grew by almost $2 T; yet, only a few in Congress recognize this issue for what it is — a threat to our national security. A bipartisan group of national security leaders like former Joint Chiefs of Staff Chairman Michael Mullen, former Defense Secretaries James Mattis and Leon Panetta, Director of National Intelligence Dan Coats, and others have warned that continued increase in our national debt will eventually hinder our ability to sustain our national security.

Reports: Former Senator Jim DeMint (R-SC) mentioned that most of the money the federal government spends is on autopilot, via entitlement programs that Congress doesn't reauthorize at all, despite full knowledge that their current spending trajectory is driving the country into insolvency.

Reports: According to the Social Security and Medicare Trustees, Social Security is facing a $13.2 T cash shortfall between 2034 and 2092. Medicare is in even worse financial shape facing a $37.7 T funding shortfall over the next 75 years. The Social Security Disability Insurance (DI) Trust Fund will be depleted in 2032, at which point the trust fund will be able to pay 96% of scheduled benefits. The Old Age and Survivors Insurance (OASI) Trust Fund will be depleted in 2034. The trust fund will be able to pay only 77% of OASI benefits.

Reports: In the final month of fiscal year 2018, the federal government spent $97 B on 509,828 contracts. On average, each contract was worth $190,190 while the largest contract was worth $2.9 B. On average, the federal government spent $3.2 B per day on contracts throughout the month of September. On September 27 and 28, spending exceeded $10 B per day.

25 March 2019. Reports: after over 1 year and 10 months of massive investigations, and more than $25 M in taxpayer funds, the Mueller report shows that there is no evidence of Russian collusion, coordination, or cooperation with the Trump campaign during the 2016 election.

Report: Boston among likeliest cities to lead world in technology in the next few years. French startups are making Boston their second home.

Reports: In February, the United States budget deficit reached an unattractive milestone, topping $234 B, the largest monthly liability on record. The latest review of these numbers by the Congressional Budget Office shows that the recent increase has been driven overwhelmingly by changes in outlays rather than revenue. The truth is, government spending has never been so unrestrained.

Reports: Bill Ford Jr., executive chairman of Ford Motor Company, expressing what many of his auto executive peers think, recently voiced frustration regarding the lack of clarity on the current administration's trade policies. But it's not just auto CEOs, chiefs across every sector have spent the past two years trying to discern what to do in the face of the randomness of the administration's trade policy — whether they agree with the goals or not.

Puerto Rico: (Population 3.6 M, rank 134, decrease 0.1%; an unincorporated territory of the United States, located in the northeast Caribbean Sea, 1,600 km southeast of Miami, Florida.).

United Nations.   There are 195 officially recognized countries. Around 44,000 people work for the United Nations. There is a wide range of jobs: Researchers, IT-specialists, lawyers, experts on finance and administration, or translators work at the New York headquarters, at the official locations, or at specialized agencies. More than half of the UN's workforce is employed in the field, in projects of humanitarian aid, or on peace missions.

Chicago, 1837: from the Skydeck (floor 103, 412 m) of Willis Tower (1973, 108 floors, 527 m) a view of the north-east part of Chicago, with Chase Tower (1969, 60 floors, 260 m, center-right down), and Lake Michigan (up).

China, Japan, and neighbors

China: (Population 1.4 B, rank 1, growth 0.4%. Freedom House reports for 2019: Not Free (15 of 100). Area 9.59 M km^2, rank 3).

5 March 2019. Reports: At the opening of China's National People's Congress, Premier Li Keqiang said the nation must be prepared for a "tough struggle", as it faces a "grave and more complicated environment." On that note, he cut the country's economic growth target this year to 6.0% - 6.5%, lower than the GDP growth of 6.6% in 2018, the slowest pace since 1990.

Reports: At Google, the censored search product for China is still ongoing, despite signs it had "effectively ended" in December. A group of employees identified around 900 changes to Dragonfly-related code over the last few months, and saw that about 100 workers were still grouped under the budget associated with the project.

Reports: 2019 China defense budget will increase by 7.5%. - China vows 'reasonable' rise in defense spending ahead of national security budget's release. As China armed forces are on the rise, India military is in alarming shape, New York Times says

6 March 2019. China Daily. Nearly 1.1 million international students are studying at universities and colleges in the United States, contributing $42 billion to the country's economy. For every seven international students enrolled, three US jobs are created and supported through tuition and other expenses.

However, the years of easy growth may be over for many of the schools, as new enrollment of international students has declined for a third consecutive year.

New student enrollments fell from the 2016-17 academic year by 6.6% for the 2017-18 period, according to a new study.

However, overall international enrollments increased by 1.5% from 2016-17 to 2017-18, according to a survey last year by the Institute of International Education in New York. It collected data from 2,075 institutions. The report also found that most of the international students are from China, with more than 363,000 enrolling in the

2017-2018 school year, or about one-third of the total international student population in the US.

At UC Berkeley, China provides the largest number of foreign students, accounting for more than 37% of the international total. In the fall, the university had 2,448 Chinese students, 169 more than at the same time the previous year, a rise of 7.42%. Tuition and fees for international undergraduates are $46,170 a year, according to the university's international office.

"Visa application process issues or visa delays/denials" is listed as the top reason for reduced new enrollment in the fall last year, according to the Institute of International Education.

Reports: Some companies have chosen not to build data centers in countries like China, that have a track record of violating human rights like privacy or freedom of expression.

Reports: Tesla has signed an agreement with lenders in China for a 12-month credit facility of up to 3.5 B yuan, or about $521 M, for its Gigafactory in Shanghai. The company broke ground on the facility in January. Tesla has estimated the Gigafactory will cost about $2 B to build, and will allow it to better compete with Chinese EV makers, by avoiding the worst of the trade tariffs.

Reports: China is infiltrating the U.S. education system in a propaganda coup.

13 March 2019. Xinhua: President Xi Jinping on Tuesday, 12 March, stressed fulfilling the set targets and tasks of national defense and military development as scheduled.

Chinese President Xi Jinping, also general secretary of the Communist Party of China (CPC) Central Committee and chairman of the Central Military Commission, meets with deputies from the People's Liberation Army (PLA) and armed police, before attending a plenary meeting of the delegation of the PLA and armed police at the second session of the 13th National People's Congress (NPC) in Beijing, capital of China, March 12, 2019. Xi delivered an important speech at the meeting on Tuesday. Xi made the remarks when attending a plenary meeting of the delegation of the People's Liberation Army (PLA) and armed police force at the second session of the 13th National People's Congress, China's national legislature. This year is the key year for completing the building of a moderately prosperous society in all respects. The entire armed forces must clearly understand the importance and urgency of implementing the

13th Five-Year Plan for military development, firm up their resolve, intensify the sense of mission, forge ahead with a pioneering spirit, and go all out to carry out the plan, so as to ensure that the set targets and tasks are fulfilled as scheduled, he said.

Xi called on the whole army to adhere to the guidance of the thought on socialism with Chinese characteristics for a new era, fully implement the Party's thinking on strengthening the military for the new era, and the military strategy for new conditions, concentrate on war preparedness, and intensify reform and innovation.

On implementation of the plan, Xi stressed that it is imperative to strengthen overall planning and coordination, as well as make breakthroughs in key areas. Xi pointed out that it is necessary to take into consideration the overall situation and coordinate the task plans, resources, and management procedures to ensure orderly advancement of various projects. Focusing on the overall layout of the plan, the military should give prominence to key projects, including urgent necessities for military preparedness, crucial support for combat systems, and coordinated projects for the reform of national defense and armed forces, he noted.

Xi stressed the formulation of the 14th Five-Year Plan for military development should serve the demands of the national development, security and military strategies, and should take into account both the actual condition, and long-term development needs.

Reports: U.S. Navy is under cyber-attack from Chinese cybercriminals, and losing national security secrets.

Reports: Mainland China wants to improve conditions for Taiwan youth to pursue education and careers in China.

20 March 2019. Xinhua: President Xi Jinping stressed firm implementation of major reforms at the seventh meeting of the central committee for deepening overall reform Tuesday, 19 March. Xi, also general secretary of the Communist Party of China (CPC) Central Committee, chairman of the Central Military Commission, and head of the central committee for deepening overall reform, presided over and addressed the meeting. Xi stressed efforts to fix the problem of formalities for formalities' sake at the grassroots level through reform, continue to strengthen people's sense of fulfillment, happiness and security, and unswervingly promote the implementation of major reform policies and measures. Members of the Standing Committee of the Political Bureau of the CPC Central

Committee and deputy heads of the reform committee Li Keqiang, Wang Huning and Han Zheng also attended the meeting.

Participants agreed that to reach a new stage in the large-scale development of the western region, measures should be taken to focus on priorities, address inadequacies, and shore up points of weakness.

The meeting decided to prioritize ecological and environmental protection, and stick to a new path featuring environmental protection, and green growth in the western region development.

With joint development of the Belt and Road playing a leading role, the country should accelerate cross-border route and regional hub construction, as well as improve the infrastructure network, for a high level of opening-up and economic development.

The meeting also stressed efforts to promote high-quality development and coordinate economic and social development of the population, resources and environment in the western region.

Stating that higher education and research institutes serve as important forces in the process of implementing the innovation-driven development strategy, and making China a country of innovators, the participants underlined efforts to streamline management procedures for science and technology projects, and reform the system on approval and enforcement of major science and technology projects.

Participants agreed that efforts should be made to promote further integration of artificial intelligence with the real economy, deepen reform and innovation, optimize the institutional environment and boost the innovation vitality of enterprises. The meeting also stressed strengthening and improving rural governance, calling for the establishment of a law-based modern rural social governance model under which Party committees exercise leadership, the government assumes responsibility, non-governmental actors provide assistance, and the public gets involved. Efforts are needed to deepen the integration and sharing of public resource trading platforms, innovate the transaction supervision system, and improve the efficiency and fairness of public resource allocation.

The meeting stressed promoting reform in the operation mechanism of the oil and natural gas pipeline network. The country will set up oil and gas pipeline network companies that are state-owned capital controlled, and with diversified investors. The country will also work to improve the oil and natural gas resource allocation efficiency and ensure a stable supply of resources.

The meeting stressed speeding up the building of a modern public legal service system that covers urban and rural areas with high efficiency, convenience, and equitable access.

As for reform on firefighting law enforcement, the meeting stressed efforts to develop new ways of regulation and supervision, strengthen management at the source, further streamline administration and delegate powers, and resolutely remove various unreasonable barriers. The participants called for efforts to defuse prominent tensions and problems, and push forward reform in a steady and orderly way, as this year will face more challenges and risks in reform and development. A number of documents were reviewed and adopted at Tuesday's meeting.

21 March 2019. Xinhua: Chinese President Xi Jinping met with president of Harvard University, Lawrence Bacow, at the Great Hall of the People in Beijing, Wednesday, 20 March, and expressed the hope that Sino-U.S. cultural and people-to-people exchanges could produce more positive results. Noting that this is Bacow first overseas visit after taking office, Xi said the tour showcases the importance attached by Bacow to Sino-U.S. education exchanges.

Xi said education exchanges and cooperation are an important part of Sino-U.S. relations, and help enhance the public opinion of the bilateral friendship. China advocates mutual learning, encourages Chinese students to study abroad, and supports education exchanges and cooperation with other countries. Xi said that he felt very happy that U.S. President Donald Trump also expressed support for bilateral cultural and people-to-people exchanges and cooperation, in their meeting in Argentina at the end of last year.

Xi stressed that over the past 40 years of reform and opening up, China's rapid development has also benefited from the improvement of education. China is committed to advancing the modernization of education and making its education system satisfying for its people. "We will expand the opening up of education, strengthen exchanges and experiences sharing with countries around the world, and jointly promote the development of education," said Xi, expressing the willingness to conduct more extensive exchanges and cooperation with U.S. educational and research institutions, such as Harvard University.

Bacow said he is visiting not only as the president of Harvard University, but also as a representative of U.S. universities, to promote education exchanges with China.

He said maintaining and deepening exchanges and cooperation, between the two countries' education and cultural institutions, is crucial to promoting U.S.-China relations in the long run. Hailing the popularity of the Chinese language at Harvard, Bacow boasted that Harvard has a large number of Chinese students. Bacow said it is admirable that the Chinese government attaches great importance to higher education, and makes huge efforts in this regard, noting that Harvard will continue to promote exchanges and cooperation with Chinese educational and scientific research institutions.

Hong Kong. (Population 7.3 M, rank 104, growth 0.8%. Partly Free: 61 of 100).

Macau (Population 622 K, rank 167, growth 1.7 %.)

Taiwan: (Population 23.6 M, rank 56, growth 0.3%. Free, 91 of 100).

27 March 2019. Xinhua: The People's Liberation Army will remain on high alert to resolutely safeguard national sovereignty and territorial integrity, a spokesperson for the Ministry of National Defense said Tuesday, 26 March.

Spokesperson Ren Guoqiang made the remarks in response to a news report that a U.S. Navy warship and a U.S. Coast Guard ship sailed through the Taiwan Strait on March 24.

"We are clear about the passage of the U.S. vessels through the Taiwan Strait and have monitored them from start to end," Ren said, adding that China had expressed concern to the U.S. side.

The Taiwan question bears on China's sovereignty and territorial integrity, and is the most important and most sensitive core issue concerning China-U.S. relations, he said. "The U.S. side should strictly abide by the one-China principle, and the three China-U.S. joint communiques, prudently handle Taiwan-related issues, and avoid damaging relations between the two countries and two militaries, as well as cross-Strait peace and stability," Ren said.

Japan: the entrance to a traditional Japanese restaurant in Inzai, 30 km northeast of Tokyo, which has a part of the restaurant being reserved for customers who prefer the Japanese tradition of seating on the floor.

Japan (Population 127.5 M, rank 11, decrease 0.2%. Free, 96 of 100).

Reports: The dark side of Japan Inc. No episode in recent memory has highlighted the reality of business in Japan as much as the ongoing abuse of Carlos Ghosn. It reminds us that the micropolitics of planned economies can be very misguided.

Reports: Japan is number 4 on the list of the world's healthiest countries.

Afghanistan: (Population 35.5 M, rank 40, growth 2.5%. Not free: 24 of 100).

South Korea: (Population 50.9 M, rank 27, growth 0.4%. Free, 82 of 100).

North Korea: (Population 25.4 M, rank 52, growth 0.5%. Not free: 3 of 100).

Vietnam (Population 95.5 M, rank 15, growth 1%. Not free, 20 of 100).

Laos (Population. 6.8 M, rank 106, growth 1.5%. Not free: 12 of 100).

Cambodia (Population 16 M, rank 71, growth 1.5%. Not Free 31 of 100).

Mongolia (Population 3 M, rank 137, growth 1.6%. Free 85 of 100)

Nepal: (Population 29.3 M, rank 48, growth 1.1%. Partly free 52 of 100).

Japan: the entrance to a traditional Japanese restaurant in Inzai, 30 km northeast of Tokyo, which has a part of the restaurant being reserved for customers who prefer the Japanese tradition of seating on the floor.

Russia, Switzerland, Eastern Europe

Russia: (Population 143.9 M, rank 9, growth 0%. Not free: 20 of 100. Area 17 M km^2, rank 1)

Switzerland: (Population 8.4 M, rank 99, growth 0.9%. Free: 96 of 100).
Reports: World's first digitally built house opens in Dübendorf, east of Zürich.
Reports: Switzerland is number 5 on the list of the world's healthiest countries.

Austria: (Population 8.7 M, rank 98, growth 0.3%. Free: 95 of 100).

Poland: (Population 38.1 M, rank 37, decrease 0.1%. Free: 89 of 100).
Reports: Command and control experts at Northrop Grumman Corp. are preparing to build two battle management systems for the government of Poland, to help military authorities quickly deal with uncertain information concerning potential air and missile attacks.

Croatia: (Population 4.1 M, rank 129, decrease 0.6%. Free: 87 of 100).

Finland: (Population 5.5 M, rank 116, growth 0.4%. Free: 100 of 100).
Reports: Finnish government collapses due to rising cost of universal health care.

Romania (Population: 19.6 M, rank 59, decrease 0.5%. Free: 84 of 100)

Moldova: (Population: 4 M, rank 132, decrease 0.2%. Partly Free: 62 of 100).

Belarus: (Population: 9.4 M, rank 93, decrease 0.1%. Not Free: 20 of 100).

Bulgaria: (Population: 7 M, rank 105, decrease 0.7%. Free: 80 of 100).

Slovenia: (Population: 2 M, rank 148, growth 0.1%. Free: 92 of 100).

Hungary: (Population: 9.7 M, rank 91, decrease 0.3%. Free: 76 of 100)

Ukraine: (Population: 44.2 M, rank 32, decrease 0.5%. Partly free: 61 of 100).

Latvia: (Population: 1.9 M, rank 150, decrease 1.1%. Free: 87 of 100).
Reports: GDP data for Q4 show that Latvia (+1.2%) recorded the third growth compared to the previous quarter.

Lithuania: (Population: 2.8 M, rank 141, decrease 0.6%. Free: 91 of 100).
Reports: GDP data for Q4 show that Lithuania (+1.3%) recorded the second growth compared to the previous quarter.

Estonia: (Population: 1.3 M, rank 155, decrease 0.2%. Free: 94 of 100).
Reports: GDP data for Q4 show that Estonia (+2.2%) recorded the highest growth compared to the previous quarter.

Serbia: (including Kosovo: Population: 8.7 M, rank 97, decrease 0.3%. Free: 76 of 100).

Kosovo ((Disputed: recognized by 110 countries, and not recognized by Serbia, Russia, and others) Population: 1.8 M, Partly free: 52 of 100).

Bosnia and Herzegovina: (Population: 3.5 M, rank 135, decrease 0.3%. Partly free: 55 of 100).

Turkey: (Population 80.7 M, rank 19, growth 1.2%. Partly free: 38 of 100).

2 April 2019. Vladimir Putin had a telephone conversation with President of the Republic of Turkey, Recep Tayyip Erdogan.

Greece: (Population 11.1 M, rank 82, decrease 0.2%. Free: 84 of 100).

Reports: GDP data for Q4 show that Greece had a decrease (-0.1%) compared to the previous quarter.

Republic of North Macedonia: (Population 2 M, rank 147, growth 0.1%. Partly Free: 57 of 100).

Albania: (Population 2.9 M, rank 139, growth 0.1%. Partly free: 68 of 100).

Cyprus: (Population 1.1 M, rank 159, growth 0.8%. Free: 94 of 100).

Kazakhstan (Population 18.2 M, rank 64, growth 1.2%. Not free: 22 of 100. Area 2.72 M km^2, rank 9.).

20 March 2019. Vladimir Putin sent a message to congratulate Kassym-Jomart Tokayev on assuming office as President of the Republic of Kazakhstan.

Armenia: (Population 2.9 M, rank 138, growth 0.2%. Partly free: 45 of 100).

Azerbaijan: (Population 9.8 M, rank 90, growth 1.1%. Not free 14 of 100).

Uzbekistan: (Population 31.9 M, rank 44, growth 1.5%. Not free: 3 of 100).

Kyrgyzstan (Population 6 M, rank 112, growth 1.5%. Partly free, 37 of 100).

28 March 2019. Vladimir Putin made a state visit to Kyrgyzstan at the invitation of President Sooronbay Jeenbekov.

Tajikistan: (Population 8.9 M, rank 96, growth 2.1%. Not free, 11 of 100).

Turkmenistan: (Population 5.7 M, rank 113, growth 1.7%. Not free, 4 of 100).

Canada: interior of Toronto Pearson International Airport (1984, 22 km northwest of downtown Toronto, in Mississauga, Ontario).

United Kingdom, Canada, South America

United Kingdom: (Population: 66.1 M, rank 21, growth 0.6%. Free: 95 of 100).

Ireland: (Population: 4.7 M, rank 123, growth 0.8%. Free: 96 of 100)

Canada: (Population: 36.6 M, rank 38, growth 0.9%. Free: 99 of 100. Area 9.9 M km², rank 2).
12 March 2019. Reports: MONTREAL, Quebec - Bombardier announced that its 7500 business jet successfully completed an 15,100 km (8,152-nautical-mile) flight non-stop, which they note is the longest mission ever flown by a purpose-built business jet. The flight took place from Singapore to Tucson, Ariz.
Reports: After leading the G7 in 2017 with growth of 3%, Canada's economic expansion slowed to 1.8% in 2018, and is expected to remain below 2% over the next two years.

Iceland: (Population: 335,000, rank 180, growth 0.8%. Free 97 of 100).
Reports: Iceland is number 3 on the list of the world's healthiest countries.

Mexico: (Population: 129.1 M, rank 10, growth 1.3%. Partly Free: 65 of 100. Area 1.96 M km², rank 13).

Chile: (Population: 18 M, rank 65, growth 0.8%. Free 94 of 100).

Colombia: (Population: 49 M, rank 29, growth 0.8%. Partly free 64 of 100).

Argentina: (Population: 44.2 M, rank 31, growth, 1%. Free: 82 of 100. Area 2.78 M km², rank 8.).

Brazil (Population: 209.2 M, rank 6, growth 0.8%. Free, 79 of 100. Area 8.5 M km², rank 5).

Reports: Brazil will sign an accord with the U.S. on space technology.

20 March 2019. Reports: As the leaders of the two largest economies in the Western Hemisphere, Presidents Trump and Jair Bolsonaro discussed yesterday, 19 March, how to increase trade and reduce barriers. They struck initial agreements on agriculture, with better access for American wheat and pork exports to Brazil, and the possibility of restarting sales of Brazilian fresh beef to the U.S.

Peru: (Population: 32.1 M, rank 5, growth 1.2%. Free: 72 of 100)

Cuba: (Population: 11.4 M, rank 42, growth 0.1%. Not free, 15 of 100).
Reports: Google works in Cuba for improved connectivity.

Bolivia: (Population: 11 M, rank 83, growth 1.5%. Partly free 68 of 100).

Paraguay: (Population: 6.8 M, rank 107, growth 1.3%. Partly free 64 of 100).

Panama: (Population: 4.1 M, rank 131, growth 1.6%. Free: 83 of 100).

Venezuela: (Population: 32 M, rank 43, growth 1.3%. Not free: 30 of 100).

Guyana: (Population 777K, (rank 165, grows 0.6%). Free: 74 of 100).

Trinidad and Tobago: (Population 1.3 M, (rank 153, grows 0.3%). Free: 81 of 100).

Nicaragua: (Population 6.2 M, (rank 110, grows 1.1%). Partly Free: 47 of 100).

El Salvador: (Population 6.3 M (rank 108, grows 0.5%). Free: 70 of 100). 2 April 2019. Reports: The U.S. is cutting off aid to El Salvador, Guatemala and Honduras, for sending migrants to the U.S. A House Appropriations Committee aide estimated that around $700 M of aid was affected.

Paris, La Seine, on Parisis boat: the east side of the Galeries des Antiques (south building) of Musée du Louvre (1793).

France, Germany, and neighbors

France: (Population 64.9 M, rank 22, growth 0.4%. Free: 90 of 100).

5 March 2019. Reports: ANGOULÃŠME, France - In order to meet the high market demand for cadet pilot training in Europe – 94,000 new pilots over the next 20 years – Airbus has decided to open its own flight academy, and extend its training services.

27 March 2019. Xinhua: Chinese President Xi Jinping on Tuesday, 26 March, urged countries around the world to make concerted efforts in four aspects and jointly shape the future of mankind, in the face of severe global challenges.

Chinese President Xi Jinping, French President Emmanuel Macron, German Chancellor Angela Merkel, and European Commission President Jean-Claude Juncker attended the closing ceremony of a global governance forum co-hosted by China and France in Paris, France, March 26, 2019.

Xi made the remarks at the closing ceremony of a global governance forum co-hosted by China and France in Paris. Besides Xi and his French counterpart, Emmanuel Macron, the event was also attended by German Chancellor Angela Merkel and European Commission President Jean-Claude Juncker. China and France, both important players in global governance, enjoy a broad political consensus and a solid foundation for cooperation on such major issues as safeguarding world peace, security and stability, upholding multilateralism and free trade, and supporting the United Nations (UN) in playing an active role, Xi said. He noted that China and France are both committed to the principles of mutual respect, mutual trust, equality, openness, inclusiveness, and win-win results. The two countries, he added, have been jointly safeguarding the fundamental principles in international relations, and advancing the improvement of global governance, and have become an important force for safeguarding world peace and stability, and promoting the advancement of human civilization. Xi proposed a four-pronged approach to addressing "four deficits" in global affairs.

Firstly, the Chinese president called for fairness and reasonableness to address the governance deficit.

It is advisable to uphold a vision of global governance featuring extensive consultation, joint contribution and shared benefits, and the principle that global affairs should be settled by the peoples of the world through consultation, Xi said, calling for actively advancing the democratization of global governance rules.

He also called for upholding the UN, a banner of multilateralism, giving full play to the constructive role of global and regional multilateral mechanisms, and jointly pushing for the building of a community with a shared future for mankind.

Secondly, Xi called for consultation and understanding to address the trust deficit. It is advisable to put mutual respect and mutual trust in the first place, make use of dialogue and consultation, seek common ground, while shelving and narrowing differences, increase strategic trust, and reduce mutual suspicion, Xi said.

It is also advisable to take a right approach to justice and interests by putting justice before interests, Xi said.

He urged closer communication and dialogue between different civilizations, so as to increase mutual understanding and mutual recognition between one another.

Thirdly, he called for joint efforts and mutual assistance to address the peace deficit. It is advisable to uphold a new vision of common, comprehensive, cooperative and sustainable security, discard Cold-War and zero-sum mentalities, reject the law of the jungle, and settle conflicts through peaceful ways, he said.

He also called for rejecting such approaches as beggaring thy neighbor, and seeking benefits at the expense of others.

Fourthly, Xi called for mutual benefit and win-win results to address the development deficit. It is advisable to pursue an innovation-driven, well-coordinated and inter-connected, and fair and inclusive approach, and forge a growth model of vitality, a cooperation model of openness and win-win results, and a development model of balance and common benefits, so that people from across the world could share the benefits of economic globalization, Xi said.

The Chinese side supports necessary UN reforms and safeguards the multilateral trading system, Xi said, adding that his country welcomes France and other countries to actively take part in the development of the Belt and Road.

He also called for joint efforts to advance the negotiations on a China-European Union (EU) investment agreement.

Hailing China-France friendship, Xi called on the two countries to strengthen cooperation with a long-term and future-oriented perspective under the new circumstances. China and France should deepen cooperation in traditional areas, accelerate cooperation in emerging areas, strengthen cooperation in addressing climate change, implement the Paris Agreement in an all-round way, and push for positive results at the UN 2019 climate summit, so as to benefit the two peoples, as well as the whole world, Xi said.

Macron said communication and coordination between the EU and China play an indispensable role in safeguarding multilateralism.

The EU and China take similar positions in such areas as the Iranian nuclear issue, climate change and Africa's security and development, and both insist on the construction of a strong and just multilateral system, he said. He said that China's fast development and poverty alleviation efforts are impressive.

France attaches importance to the significant and active role played by China in international affairs, he said. The EU and China, as important forces on the world stage, should increase strategic mutual trust and promote cooperation through dialogue, he said.

The Belt and Road Initiative (BRI) proposed by China is significant, and can play an important role in world peace, stability and development, he said. The EU could align its development strategy with the BRI in an innovative way, and jointly promote Eurasian connectivity, he added.

Merkel said the sound relationship between European countries and China has laid a good foundation for carrying out multilateral cooperation between the EU and China. The EU should accelerate the negotiations on the EU-China investment agreement, and actively discuss participation in the BRI, she said.

The EU and China should cooperate to safeguard multilateralism and compare notes on reforms of the World Trade Organization (WTO), and other multilateral institutions, she said.

Germany, she said, proposes to hold a leaders' meeting between the EU and China next year.

Referring to the EU and China as important strategic cooperative partners, Juncker said it is important that the two sides maintain dialogue on an equal footing.

He called for the EU and China to actively advance the negotiations on the EU-China investment agreement, and maintain coordination on major international issues, such as WTO reforms.

Juncker said he is looking forward to seeing positive results at the upcoming EU-China leaders' meeting.

Belgium (Population 11.4 M, rank 80, growth 0.6%. Free: 95 of 100).

European Commission, European Union, EU: 28 EU countries: Austria, Belgium, Bulgaria, Croatia, Republic of Cyprus, Czech Republic, Denmark, Estonia, Finland, France, Germany, Greece, Hungary, Ireland, Italy, Latvia, Lithuania, Luxembourg, Malta, Netherlands, Poland, Portugal, Romania, Slovakia, Slovenia, Spain, Sweden and the UK.

27 March 2019. Xinhua: The UN Security Council members from the European Union said Tuesday, 26 March, that they do not recognize Israel's sovereignty over the occupied Golan Heights.

The five members -- Belgium, Britain, France, Germany, and Poland -- issued a joint statement after U.S. President Donald Trump's Monday, 25 March, proclamation to recognize Israel's sovereignty over the territory that Israel seized from Syria in 1967, and annexed in 1981. "Our position on the status of the Golan Heights is well-known, and we would like to make it clear that this position has not changed. In line with international law, and relevant Security Council resolutions, notably Resolutions 242 and 497, we do not recognize Israel's sovereignty over the territories occupied by Israel since June 1967, including the Golan Heights, and we do not consider them to be part of the territory of the State of Israel," said the statement, which was read out to reporters by Belgian UN ambassador Marc Pecsteen de Buytswerve. "Annexation of territory by force is prohibited under international law. Any declaration of a unilateral border change goes against the foundation of the rules-based international order and the UN Charter."

The EU members of the Security Council also raised strong concerns about broader consequences of recognizing illegal annexation, and about the broader regional consequences.

Germany: (Population 82.1 M, rank 16, growth 0.2%. Free: 95 of 100).

27 March 2019. Xinhua: Chinese President Xi Jinping meets with German Chancellor Angela Merkel on the sidelines of a global governance forum co-hosted by China and France in Paris, France, March 26, 2019.

Chinese President Xi Jinping met with German Chancellor Angela Merkel in Paris on Tuesday, 26 March, and put forward a three-point proposal on the further development of China-Germany relations.

The two leaders met on the sidelines of a global governance forum co-hosted by China and France.

China-Germany practical cooperation has maintained a sound momentum of development, despite an increase of volatility and uncertainty in the current international situation, Xi said.

China was Germany's largest trading partner for a third consecutive year in 2018, with a nearly 140% increase in German companies' actual investment in China, he said. China, Xi told Merkel, has set its goals and ideas that it would continue to deepen reform, expand opening-up, and promote high-quality economic development.

Noting that China stands firm in sticking to opening-up, Xi said China is also sincere in advancing and expanding its cooperation with Germany and with the European Union (EU).

China is willing to join efforts with Germany to continue to expand and consolidate the basis of China-Germany cooperation, so as to bring more benefits to the two peoples, he said.

Recalling that Merkel has repeatedly expressed her firm belief in win-win cooperation, the president said China also considers joint cooperation, mutual benefits and win-win results the only right choice in resolving various global problems.

Under the current circumstances, the significance of strengthening China-Germany and China-EU cooperation is beyond the bilateral scope, Xi said, putting forward a three-point proposal on the next-stage development of China-Germany ties.

Firstly, the two countries should deepen their bilateral cooperation to set an example of win-win cooperation for the world, Xi said.

Noting that China and Germany are not rivals nor adversaries, Xi said seeking win-win results through cooperation is the main thread in China-Germany ties, and urged the two sides to boost cooperation in such fields as artificial intelligence, automatic driving, new materials, new energy, life sciences and smart city. Xi said he hopes that Germany would create a friendly and open policy environment for Chinese enterprises to invest and develop in Germany.

Secondly, the Chinese president proposed that the two countries take the lead in China-EU cooperation to inject more stability into the world. China sees Europe as an important force in promoting world multipolarization, and has always been a staunch supporter for Europe's path of unity and self-improvement, Xi said.

With China and Europe being the world's two major forces of stability and two major economies, the steady growth of their relations conforms to the common interests of both sides, and is conducive to increasing stability in the complex and ever-changing world today, he said. China hopes that Germany would exert an important and positive influence on helping the EU to focus on cooperation and avoid disturbance, he added.

Thirdly, the two countries should jointly advance global governance to safeguard multilateralism, Xi said.

China is willing to work with Germany to uphold the international system with the United Nations at its core, he said, urging the two sides to enhance coordination within the framework of the Group of Twenty, to make greater contributions to improving global economic governance. The Belt and Road Initiative is conducive to promoting international economic cooperation, and building an open world economy, Xi told Merkel, pledging to expand third-party cooperation with the German side.

Merkel said Germany and China share broad common interests, with sound development of bilateral ties in recent years, and close communication and cooperation at all levels and in various fields.

Germany would like to deepen its economic and trade relations with China in the digital age, and is willing to actively participate in the second Belt and Road Forum for International Cooperation, Merkel said. Germany is looking forward to fully utilizing the market opportunities brought by China's further opening-up, and will provide a fair and favorable market environment for Chinese enterprises to invest and start business in Germany, she said.

The chancellor noted that her country is committed to promoting EU-China cooperative relations, and stands for joint efforts of the EU and China in safeguarding multilateralism.

Xi arrived in Paris from the southern French city of Nice on Monday, 25 March, to continue his state visit to France.

France is the final stop of Xi's three-nation Europe tour, which has already taken him to Italy and Monaco.

Norway (Population 5.3 M, rank 118, growth 1%. Free: 100 of 100).

Reports: Norway is number 9 on the list of the world's healthiest countries.

Sweden (Population 9.9 M, rank 89, growth 0.7%. Free: 100 of 100).

Reports: GDP data for Q4 show that Sweden (+1.2%) recorded the third growth compared to the previous quarter.

Reports: Sweden is number 6 on the list of the world's healthiest countries.

The Netherlands (Population 17 M, rank 67, growth 0.3%. Free: 99 of 100).

Czech Republic (Population 10.6 M, rank 87, growth 0.1%. Free: 94 of 100).

26 March 2019. Reports: Last week, the Leipzig Book Fair celebrated reading. 286,000 visitors visited the most important German literary fair, in addition to the Frankfurt Book Fair, and were inspired by new publications on the book market. Guest country this year was the Czech Republic. Right at the entrance of the fair there was a sculpture that visualized the fall of the Berlin wall in Germany thirty years ago, and the political events in Central and Eastern Europe. A development with consequences for the literary world, too. 1989 also meant a radical change for the Czech literary scene: intellectual exchange across borders was henceforth possible, access to books was unlimited and open to all.

Denmark (Population 5.7 M, rank 114, growth 0.4%. Free: 97 of 100. Area (including Greenland) 2.22 M km^2, rank 12 but not official).

5 March 2019. Reports: COPENHAGEN, Denmark – Cobham SATCOM announced that it would provide L-band ground

infrastructure for Inmarsat's I-6 constellation, currently set for first launch in 2020.

Luxembourg (Population 583 K, rank 169, growth 1.3%. Free: 98 of 100).

Spain: (Population 46.3 M, rank 30, growth 0%. Free: 94 of 100).

Reports: Spain is number 1 on the list of the world's healthiest countries.

Portugal: (Population 10.3 M, rank 88, decrease 0.4%. Free: 97 of 100).

Reports: Portugal picks glass cockpit avionics from Collins Aerospace for C-130H Hercules aircraft modernization.

Liechtenstein: (Population: 38,000, rank 215, growth 0.7%, Free: 91 of 100)

UK, Cambridge: From Clare Bridge (1640, 1969) over River Cam, looking north to the Garret Hostel Bridge (center back), Punting Cambridge (center right), Trinity Hall Garden (right), Clare Fellows Garden (left).

India, Pakistan, Australia, and neighbors

India (Population: 1.3 B, rank 2nd, growth 1.1%. Free: 77 of 100. Area 3.28 M km^2, rank 7).

5 March 2019. Reports: The U.S. administration has decided goods from India and Turkey are no longer eligible for preferential, tariff-free access to the U.S. market. India has currently been exporting $5.6 B worth of goods to the U.S. duty free under the GSP program.

Indonesia: (Population: 263.9 M, rank 4, growth 1.1%. Partly free: 65 of 100. Area 1.91 M km^2, rank 14.).

Australia: (Population: 24.4 M, rank 53, growth 1.3%. Free: 98 of 100. Area 7.69 M km^2, rank 6).

6 March 2019. Reports: Australia reported lower than expected growth last year, as it battled a steep housing downturn, lackluster consumer spending, and trade challenges with slower growth in China. Annual GDP expanded 2.3%, the slowest since mid-2017, and below expectations for a 2.5% increase.

Reports: Australia is number 7 on the list of the world's healthiest countries.

19 March 2019. Reports: In a letter to Japan's Shinzo Abe, Australian Prime Minister Scott Morrison asked the G20 chair to make platform monitoring central to the world leaders' upcoming summit in Osaka in June. "It is unacceptable to treat the internet as an ungoverned space," he said. Facebook confirmed yesterday that a live-streamed video showing last week's New Zealand mosque attacks was viewed 4,000 times before it was removed.

New Zealand: (Population 4.7 M, rank 125, growth 1%. Free: 98 of 100.

15 March 2019. Vladimir Putin sent Prime Minister of New Zealand a message of condolences in the wake of the tragic terrorist attack in the city of Christchurch.

Pakistan: (Population 212 M, rank 5, growth 2%. Partly free: 43 of 100).

Philippines: (Population 104.9 M, rank 13, growth 1.5%. Partly free 63 of 100).

Singapore: (Population 5.7 M, rank 115, growth 1.5%. Partly free 51 of 100).

The EAS currently comprises 18 countries: 10 ASEAN members (Brunei Darussalam, Cambodia, Indonesia, Laos, Malaysia, Myanmar, the Philippines, Singapore, Thailand and Vietnam), and eight dialogue partners: Russia (joined the EAS in 2010), the United States, Japan, South Korea, India, China, Australia and New Zealand.

APEC (21 members: Singapore, China, USA, Vietnam, Australia, Japan, Indonesia, Russia, Philippines, Malaysia, Hong Kong, Thailand, Chile, Canada, New Zealand, South Korea, Peru, Mexico, Brunei, Papua New Guinea, Chinese Taipei)

Reports: Singapore is number 8 on the list of the world's healthiest countries.

Thailand: (Population 69 M, rank 20, growth 0.3%. Not free 32 of 100).

Myanmar (Burma, Population 53.3 M, rank 26, growth 0.9%. Not free 32 of 100

Bangladesh (Population 164.6 M, rank 8, growth 1.1%. Partly free 47 of 100).

Sri Lanka (Population 20.8 M, rank 58, growth 0.4%. Partly free 56 of 100).

Malaysia (Population 31.6 M, rank 45, growth 1.34%. Partly free 44 of 100).

Brunei: (Population 428,000, rank 176, growth 1.3%. Not free 29 of 100).

Vanuatu: (Population 276,000, rank 185, growth 2.2%. Free 80 of 100)

Tonga: (Population 108,000, rank 195, growth 0.8%. Free 74 of 100

Papua New Guinea: (Population 8.2 M, rank 101, growth 2.1%, Partly Free 64 of 100). APEC (21 members: Singapore, China, USA, Vietnam, Australia, Japan, Indonesia, Russia, Philippines, Malaysia, Hong Kong, Thailand, Chile, Canada, New Zealand, South Korea, Peru, Mexico, Brunei, Papua New Guinea, Chinese Taipei)

Paris: A Lamborghini supercar (Automobili Lamborghini, 1963, Italy), in the east part of Place de la Concorde, near Tuileries Gardens.

Italy, Middle East, Africa

Italy: (Population 59.3 M, rank 23, decrease 0.1%. Free: 89 of 100).

6 March 2019. Reports: Italy plans to sign a memorandum of understanding to become a part of China's Belt and Road Initiative by the end of March, marking the first endorsement by a G7 nation, FT reports. The support would likely undermine Brussels' efforts to overcome divisions within the EU over the best approach to deal with Chinese investments.

Reports: GDP data for Q4 show that Italy had a decrease (-0.1%) compared to the previous quarter.

Reports: Italy is number 2 on the list of the world's healthiest countries.

23 March 2019. Xinhua: Chinese President Xi Jinping and his Italian counterpart Sergio Mattarella hold talks in Rome, Italy, March 22, 2019. Chinese President Xi Jinping and his Italian counterpart, Sergio Mattarella, held talks here in Rome, Friday, 22 March, and agreed to jointly push for greater development of the China-Italy comprehensive strategic partnership in the new era.

The two heads of state agreed to guide the direction of bilateral ties from a strategic height, and long-term perspective.

During their talks, Xi noted that both, as countries with an ancient civilization, China and Italy have profound historical relations.

This year marks the 15th anniversary of the China-Italy comprehensive strategic partnership, and the two countries will celebrate the 50th anniversary of their diplomatic relations next year, Xi said. He recalled that for nearly half a century, China and Italy have respected, trusted and helped each other, enhanced high-level exchanges and strategic mutual trust, facilitated communication, cooperation and convergence of interests, and deepened mutual understanding and traditional friendship.

As the world is undergoing profound changes unseen in a century, China is willing to carry forward the spirit of cooperation with the Italian side, strengthen strategic communication, encourage the international community to seek common ground, while reserving differences, and promote development through cooperation, so as to contribute new wisdom and strength to building a better world, Xi said. China stands ready to join hands with Italy to firmly keep the direction of bilateral relations in the new era, carry out closer high-level exchanges, and upgrade the quality and level of bilateral practical cooperation, he said. Xi said he agrees with Mattarella that Italy and China should be partners with inclusive interests and common development, adding that China is willing to enhance the comprehensive strategic partnership with Italy. The two sides need to strengthen communication on visions, consolidate political mutual trust, continue to extend mutual understanding and support on issues of each other's core interests and major concerns, and strengthen communication and cooperation between their governments, legislative bodies and political parties, Xi said.

He encouraged the two sides to create highlights in bilateral cooperation, jointly build the Belt and Road, and promote the synergy of their development strategies, and the planning of practical cooperation. China is willing to import more high-quality products from Italy, and encourage more capable Chinese enterprises to invest and start business in Italy, Xi said.

He also urged the two countries to boost cultural and people-to-people exchanges, and enhance communication and cooperation in such fields as culture, education, film and television, and media, so as to consolidate the popular support for friendship between the two peoples. On China-Europe relations, Xi said his country has always supported the European integration, and respected the European Union's efforts in solving its problems. Xi said he hopes that Italy will continue playing a positive role in promoting EU-China partnership for peace, growth, reform and civilization, Xi said.

China is willing to strengthen communication and coordination with the Italian side on major issues such as the United Nations affairs, global governance, climate change and the 2030 Agenda for Sustainable Development, jointly promote trade and investment liberalization and facilitation, and jointly push economic globalization in the direction of becoming more open, inclusive, balanced, win-win, and beneficial to all, he said.

Mattarella warmly welcomed Xi, saying he still has a vivid memory of his visit to China in 2017. The frequent high-level exchanges between Italy and China, especially President Xi's visit this time, demonstrated the high level of bilateral relations, Mattarella said, calling China a close and important partner of Italy.

Italy admires China's development achievements, appreciates China's adherence to the opening-up strategy, and has confidence in the prospect of Italy-China cooperation, he said.

Italy is willing to take the opportunities of the 15th anniversary of the Italy-China comprehensive strategic partnership this year, and the 50th anniversary of Italy-China diplomatic relations next year, to expand the mutually beneficial cooperation in various fields, such as economy and trade, investment, science and technology, and innovation between the two countries, Mattarella said.

Italy and China were at the two ends of the ancient Silk Road, which had been a bond closely linking the two countries, Mattarella said.

Italy supports Xi's initiative on jointly building the Belt and Road, and believes that it will be conducive to Eurasian connectivity and common development, as well as to reviving the ancient Silk Road in modern times, Mattarella said.

Calling the Belt and Road a cultural exchange road, the Italian president said his country is willing to boost communication and cooperation with China in culture and tourism.

Both as countries with an ancient civilization, Mattarella said the peoples of Italy and China have wisdom to address the challenges facing human society today. Italy believes that China's rejuvenation will make new historic contributions to the world's peace and prosperity, he said, adding that Italy is committed to promoting in-depth development of EU-China ties.

Italy is willing to enhance communication and coordination with China in multilateral institutions such as the UN and the Group of Twenty, jointly safeguard multilateralism and trade liberalization, and meet challenges such as climate change and international security together, Mattarella said.

The two presidents held a joint press conference after the talks.

Before their talks, the Italian president held a grand welcoming ceremony for Xi.

The Chinese president arrived in Rome Thursday, 21 March, for a state visit to Italy, the first stop of his three-nation Europe tour, which will also take him to Monaco and France.

23 March 2019. Xinhua: Chinese President Xi Jinping and his Italian counterpart Sergio Mattarella meet with representatives attending the meetings of the China-Italy Entrepreneur Committee,

China-Italy Third Party Market Cooperation Forum, and China-Italy Cultural Cooperation Mechanism in Rome, Italy, March 22, 2019.

Chinese President Xi Jinping on Friday, 22 March, urged personages of business and cultural circles in China and Italy to contribute more wisdom and strength to the cooperation between the two countries.

Xi made the remarks when speaking to representatives attending the meetings of the China-Italy Entrepreneur Committee, China-Italy Third Party Market Cooperation Forum, and China-Italy Cultural Cooperation Mechanism, which are being held in parallel in Rome. While offering congratulations on the simultaneous convening of the three institutional meetings for the first time, that showcases the China-Italy practical cooperation, Xi thanked the personages of business and cultural circles from the two countries for their long-time efforts and contributions to promote bilateral economic and trade cooperation, deepen mutual understanding between the two peoples, and enhance the friendship between the two countries.

Xi said that China and Italy both boast a time-honored history and highly value carrying forward their own civilization, which lay the foundation for the two countries to enjoy mutual understanding and lasting friendship. He praised the China-Italy relations as being strategic partners featuring mutual respect and trust, cooperative partners featuring mutual benefit and win-win result, and cultural exchange partners featuring mutual learning.

China and Italy enjoy a solid political foundation for bilateral exchanges and cooperation, as the two sides can accommodate each other's core interests and major concerns, Xi said. The two-way trade has developed steadily and the bilateral investment has grown rapidly, bringing tangible benefits to the two peoples, he said.

On cultural front, the two countries have witnessed splendid exchanges, taking the lead in cultural exchanges and cooperation between China and the West, he said.

"I am full of confidence in the prospect of the development of China-Italy relations," the Chinese president said.

Xi noted that as next year marks the 50th anniversary of China-Italy diplomatic ties, the two sides will hold year of culture and tourism in each other's country, and they will embrace new opportunities in cooperation in various areas.

China stands ready to work with all walks of life in Italy to push for a steady and long-term development of the bilateral relations on the path of mutual benefit and win-win result, and to make new contributions to boost the China-Europe connectivity and global development and prosperity at large, Xi said.

"I hope that personages of business and cultural circles in China and Italy contribute more wisdom and strength in your own fields to the cooperation between our two countries," he told the representatives. Italian President Sergio Mattarella, who also spoke at the meeting with the representatives, agreed that both Italy and China are countries with an ancient civilization, which is the root of their profound relations. The two countries enjoy a traditional friendship and a long history of trade and cultural exchanges, he said, noting that under the new circumstances, the Italian government supports the business community of the two countries in deepening economic, trade and investment cooperation, and supports cultural circles in carrying out all-ranging exchanges.

The two sides should work together to elevate their economic and trade cooperation to a new level, and expand cooperation on cultural Silk Road, in a bid to bring greater benefits to the two peoples, jointly respond to the challenges facing the world today, and lift the bilateral ties to a new height, he added.

Xi arrived in Rome Thursday, 21 March, for a state visit to Italy, the first stop of Xi's three-nation Europe tour, which will also take him to Monaco and France.

Vatican: (Population 792, rank 233 (last), decrease 1.1%).

San Marino: (Population 33,400, rank 218, growth 0.6%. Free 97 of 100)

Malta (Population 431,000, rank 175, growth 0.3%. Free, 96 of 100).

13 March 2019. Reports: Another EU nation may be joining China's Belt and Road Initiative: Malta. "You have to be careful, but for a country to survive and to be competitive, especially a small country, we need to have diversification," said Edward Scicluna, Malta's finance minister. Earlier this month, Italy - the eurozone's

third-largest economy - signaled its interest in joining the Chinese plan.

Jordan (Population 9.7 M, rank 92, growth 2.6%. Partly free, 37 of 100).

Lebanon: (Population: 6 M, rank 111, growth 1.3%. Partly free: 44 of 100).
26 March 2019. Vladimir Putin held talks at the Kremlin with President of the Lebanese Republic, Michel Aoun, who is in Russia on an official visit.

United Arab Emirates (UAE) (Population: 9.4 M, rank 94, growth 1.4%. Not free, 20 of 100. Capital: Abu Dhabi).

Saudi Arabia (Population 32.9 M, rank 41, growth 2.1%. Not free: 10 of 100. Area 2.149 M km^2, rank 12.).
5 March 2019. Reports: The Kingdom of Saudi Arabia will receive THAAD, which is regarded as America's crown jewel in missile defense systems. The multi-million-dollar award is the first installment of what is expected to be a $15 B deal.

Yemen (Population 28.2 M, rank 50, growth 2.4%. Not free: 14 of 100).

Iraq (Population 38.2 M, rank 36, growth 2.9%. Not free: 27 of 100).

Iran: (Population 81.1 M, rank 18, growth 1.1%. Not free: 17 of 100).

Israel: (Population 8.3 M, rank 100, growth 1.6%. Free: 80 of 100).
5 March 2019. Reports: The U.S. deployed THAAD in Israel for the first time in order to "deal with near and distant threats from throughout the Middle East".
2 April 2019. Vladimir Putin had a telephone conversation with Prime Minister of Israel Benjamin Netanyahu, at the Israeli side's initiative. The two leaders discussed topical issues concerning

bilateral cooperation, including military contacts, as well as the situation in the Middle East.

Palestine: (Population 4.9 M (rank 121, grows 2.7%). Not free: 28 of 100).

Egypt (Population 97.5 M (rank 14, grows 1.9%). Not free, 26 of 100).

League of Arab States (LAS) (22 countries: Algeria, Bahrein, Comoros, Djibouti, Egypt, Iraq, Jordan, Kuwait, Lebanon, Libya, Mauritania, Morocco, Oman, Palestine, Qatar, Saudi Arabia, Somalia, Sudan, Syria, Tunisia, United Arab Emirates and Yemen).
2 April 2019. Vladimir Putin sent his greetings to heads of state and government of the League of Arab States (LAS) member states on the opening of LAS Summit in Tunis, Tunisia.

Qatar: (Population 2.6 M (rank 142, grows 2.7%). Not free: 26 of 100).

Kuwait: (Population 4.1 M (rank 130, grows 2.1%). Partly free: 36 of 100).
Reports: Electronic warfare (EW) experts at Harris Corp. will provide sophisticated EW systems to the government of Kuwait that are designed to protect combat aircraft from incoming radar-guided missiles.

Oman: (Population 4.6 M (rank 127, grows 4.8%). Not free: 25 of 100)

Bahrain: (Population 1.5 M (rank 152, grows 4.7%). Not free: 12 of 100).

Syria: (Population 18.2 M (rank 63, decrease 0.9%). Not free: 0 of 100).

Kenya: (Population 49.7 M (rank 28, growth 2.6%. Partly free, 51 of 100).

Libya: (Population 6.3 M, rank 109, growth 1.3%. Not free: 13 of 100).

Algeria: (Area 2.38 M km^2, rank 10.)

Tunisia: (Population 11.5 M, rank 78, growth 1.1%. Free: 78 of 100).

Morocco: (Population 35.7 M, rank 39, growth 1.3%. Partly free: 41 of 100).

South Africa: (Population 56.7 M, rank 25, growth 1.3%. Free, 78 of 100).

Zimbabwe: (Population 16.5 M, rank 70, growth 2.4%. Partly Free, 32 of 100).

Sudan (Population 40.5 M, rank 35, growth 2.4%. Not Free: 6 of 100).

South Sudan (Population 12.5 M, rank 76, growth 2.8%. Not Free: 4 of 100)

Guinea: (Population 12.7 M, rank 75, growth 2.6%. Partly Free, 41 of 100).

Djibouti (Population 957,000, rank 160, growth 1.6%. Not Free: 26 of 100).

Somalia: (Population 14.7 M, rank 74, growth 3%. Not free: 5 of 100).

Niger (Population 21.4 M, rank 57, growth 3.9%. Partly free: 49 of 100).

Nigeria (Population 190.8 M, rank 7, growth 2.6%. Partly free: 50 of 100).

Cameroon (Population 24 M, rank 55, growth 2.6%. Not free: 24 of 100).

Sierra Leone: (Population 7.5 M (rank 103, grows 2.2%). Partly free: 66 of 100)

Chad: (Population 15 M (rank 73, grows 3.1%). Not free: 18 of 100).

The Gambia: (Population 2.1 M (rank 146, grows 3%). Not free: 20 of 100).

Malawi: (Population 18.6 M (rank 61, grows 2.9%). Partly free: 63 of 100).

Rwanda: (Population 12.2 M (rank 77, grows 2.4%). Not free: 24 of 100).

Burkina Faso: (Population 19.1 M (rank 60, grows 2.9%). Partly free: 63 of 100).

Central African Republic: (Population 4.6 M (rank 126, grows 1.4%). Not free: 10 of 100).

Senegal: (Population 15.8 M (rank 72, grows 2.8%). Free: 78 of 100).

Gabon: (Population 2 M (rank 149, grows 2.3%). Partly Free: 32 of 100).

Madagascar: (Population 25.5 M (rank 51, grows 2.7%). Partly Free: 56 of 100).

Democratic Republic of the Congo: (Population 81.3 M (rank 17, grows 3.3%). Not Free: 19 of 100. Area 2.34 M km^2, rank 11).

Angola: (Population 29.7 M (rank 46, grows 3.4%). Not Free: 24 of 100).

Zambia: (Population 17 M (rank 66, grows 3%). Partly Free: 56 of 100).

United Republic of Tanzania: (Population 57 M (rank 24, grows 3.1%). Partly Free: 58 of 100).

Ethiopia: (Population 105 M (rank 12, grows 2.5%). Not Free: 12 of 100).

10 March 2019. Vladimir Putin sent a message of condolences to President of Ethiopia, Sahle-Work Zewde, and Prime Minister of Ethiopia, Abiy Ahmed, in connection with the crash of a passenger aircraft outside Addis Ababa on 10 March.

USA, Boston: a view of the north part of Boston, from Cambridge, over Charles River Basin. The tall building is Hancock Place (241 m) in Copley Square. To the right is The Westin Copley Place Boston Hotel, and then Boston Marriott Copley Place Hotel. To the left are Trinity Church and hotels. Storrow Drive is by Charles River.

Medical

New research revealed how a bacterium in dental plaque-- involved in 1/3 of colon cancer cases-- speeds up colon cancer growth and makes the disease more deadly. – Columbia University Irving Medical Center, EMBO Reports

The field of neoantigen targeting is set to grow, with drug developers seeing more proof-of-concept clinical studies over the past year, resulting in increasingly effective personalized cancer vaccines and cell therapies.

Researchers say that understanding how frogs fight off fungal infections could lead to new treatments for humans.

Specialists created a new method that could rapidly detect cancer in cells.

6 March 2019. Reports: The FDA has approved the first drug to treat depression in decades - Johnson & Johnson will sell a nasal spray based on ketamine. Esketamine, which will be sold under the brand name Spravato, will be available for adults who have already tried at least two other antidepressant treatments. The fast-acting drug will cost between $590 and $885 (before discounts and rebates) depending on the dosage.

Scientists have discovered a technique similar to medieval stained glass-making, to make bacteria-killing glass, which can completely eradicate the deadliest hospital infections within hours.

Researchers at UC San Diego School of Medicine generated a new mouse model that mimics human acne for the first time, and used it to validate the concept of "good" and "bad" acne bacteria, and introduce new possibilities for targeted treatment.
– University of California San Diego Health, JCI Insight

Tai chi can improve balance and coordination (including in people with Parkinson's disease), memory, and sleep, as well as reduce anxiety, depression, falls, and knee, back, and other types of chronic pain.

Scientists discovered that a seawater bacterium provides leads to fight melanoma.

Of the 30 millions of Americans with diabetes, 90% to 95% have type 2, according to the Centers for Disease Control and Prevention. New research shows building muscle strength may be one way to lower risk for the disease, by as much as 32%.
– Iowa State University, Mayo Clinic Proceedings

Researchers from the Duke Eye Center have shown that a new, non-invasive imaging device can see signs of Alzheimer's disease in a matter of seconds. – American Academy of Ophthalmology (AAO), Ophthalmology Retina

Researchers used added-manufacturing to create efficient live cells.

A gene was identified, that increases the risk of antibiotic reaction.

More than 3,600,000 Americans, older than age 40, are visually impaired. And somewhere in the world, another person goes blind every five seconds. Age-related eye conditions include farsightedness, glaucoma, cataracts, macular degeneration, eyelid problems, and dry eyes.

As cancer therapies shift from targeting the tumor to targeting the immune system, choosing the right immunocompetent preclinical models is important.

University of North Carolina School of Medicine scientists uncovered a possible reason why some breast cancers are so aggressive and difficult to treat: an enzyme called USP21 promotes proliferation of basal-like breast cancer. Cell Reports

Lightweight exoskeleton provides independent mobility for disabled people.

Researchers work to find when a cell's 'fingerprint' can be a weapon against cancer.

FDA approved Dupixent for moderate-to-severe atopic dermatitis in adolescents.

A synthetic DNA structure was used as bait to capture nucleic proteins, revealing previously unknown role of the new gene repair protein HNRNPD in the cellular response to DNA damage. – Sbarro Health Research Organization (SHRO) Nucleic Acids Research

FDA approved a new generic Valsartan

Researchers observed that targeting stem-like cells could prevent ovarian cancer recurrence.

Specialists are working for solutions that can reduce, eliminate or inactivate Aflatoxins in protein milk, a specific product of a starch biorefinery process.

Reports: The world's healthiest countries are: Spain, Italy, Iceland, Japan, Switzerland, Sweden, Australia, Singapore and Norway.

Researchers observed that common heartburn medications are connected to kidney disease and failure.

Sage Therapeutics - the FDA approved the first postpartum depression drug called Zulresso. It will be available only through a restricted program requiring administration by a healthcare provider in a certified facility.

The FDA issued warning letters to Sientra and Johnson & Johnson for failing to comply with the post-approval study requirements for their breast implants.

March 30 is the National Doctors' Day.

Researchers observed that increases in chronic inflammation is the main reason why injured bones do not heal as well with age, not only the passage of time.

Scientists are looking for the brain circuit responsible for alcohol cravings.

A significant factor to the common cancer pathway was discovered. Researchers report the discovery of an unexpected regulator of the p53, opening the door to the development of drugs that could target it.

The oral cavity is host to more than 700 species of bacteria, along with other microorganisms, some protective and some potentially harmful. A study observed that heavy alcohol drinkers had an overabundance of potentially pathogenic bacteria (including *Actinomyces* and *Neisseria*), linked, for example, to endocarditis (inflammation of the heart's inner lining). Heavier drinking was associated with greater shifts in bacterial populations. Alcohol in mouthwash kills "germs" that cause plaque and gum disease.

A study explaining side effects of statins also helped cellular chemists to discover that the statins can have unexpected benefits.

Researchers from The University of Manchester observed that a new class of drugs could treat ovarian cancer.

Allergan announced the FDA approval of AVYCAZ for the treatment of complicated intra-abdominal infections in pediatric patients

Aging well is an important objective of the health organizations from many countries.

Czech specialists in cell therapy increased survival in ovarian cancer by 62%.

The FDA approved Zulresso injection for intravenous use for the treatment of postpartum depression in adult women.

Specialists improved drug release by taking control over encapsulation.

Schizophrenia is a highly complex mental disorder, with unknown causes, and no cure. Researchers are working on new experiments, which may suggest alternatives for the treatment of schizophrenia.

Research has shown that overweight men are more likely to develop benign prostatic hyperplasia (BPH) than their normal-weight counterparts.

A lifetime of walking, standing, lifting and twisting causes significant low back pain in 80% of all adults.

A pharmaceutical company announced that FDA approved Sunosi for excessive daytime sleepiness

Chemistry researchers have patented a method for making anti-leukemia compounds that until now have only been available via an Asian tree that produces them.

It is well known that air pollution contributes to many health problems, including heart disease, asthma, and other respiratory disorders. But evidence is accumulating that it can also harm the brain, especially as people age, contributing to cognitive decline and dementia.

Drug development takes an average of 10 -15 years, and 90% of drugs fail clinical development.

A combination of two topical creams lowers the risk that patients will later develop squamous cell carcinoma of the skin.

SSRIs are the most commonly prescribed medication for depression, yet scientists still do not understand why the treatment does not always work.

Scientists have connected powerful data analysis tools, and three-dimensional studies of genomic geography, to implicate new risk genes for osteoporosis.

Bacteria must travel the world by air, according to a new theory proposed by an international team of scientists.

For some men, new laser therapies offer relief for prostate enlargement, with fewer side effects.

New research suggests a hormone released from fat tissue is critical in the development of obesity-related asthma.

Researchers study unique prostate cancer tumor homograft models, for combination therapy and immunotherapy development.

A new handheld device, that combines CRISPR technology with graphene-based electronic transistors, can rapidly detect specific genetic mutations.

The FDA approved Mayzent tablets to treat adults with relapsing forms of multiple sclerosis.

A frontline chemotherapy drug is made less effective, because similar compounds, released by tumor-associated immune cells, block the drug's action.

Major depression, obesity and chronic pain are all linked to the effects of one protein, called FKBP51. Researchers have now developed a highly selective compound that can effectively block FKBP51 in mice. – American Chemical Society (ACS), *American Chemical Society (ACS) Spring 2019 National Meeting & Exposition*

In a study that will be published April 1 in the Journal of Experimental Medicine, researchers from the Institut Pasteur and INSERM reveal that chimeric antigen receptor (CAR) T cells can induce tumor regression. – The Rockefeller University Press *Journal of Experimental Medicine, May 2019; 864.12.013*

A good night's sleep may someday be more achievable by the data generated by your sleepwear. Researchers have developed pajamas embedded with self-powered sensors that provide unobtrusive and continuous monitoring. – American Chemical Society (ACS), *American Chemical Society (ACS) Spring 2019 National Meeting & Exposition*

As we age, our cognitive abilities tend to decline. It's unfortunate, but normal. Now, a study of about 5,200 cognitively normal, older people living in England, shows that this decline is more rapid in individuals with elevated blood sugar levels.

Data from two major trials show pembrolizumab benefited patients with advanced small cell lung cancer.

Glowing tumors show scientists where cancer drugs are working.

Mathematics, Science & Artificial Intelligence (AI)

Reports: The future of American consumer electronics, electric vehicles, and renewable energy will depend upon securing sources of vital minerals for battery production. Th U.S. have already fallen far behind China and other countries in its ability to securely source the vital materials that a technological future demands. A new type of fuel cell that runs off of an aqueous borohydride solution gets a big boost.

New battery research may result in high-performance batteries made entirely from polymeric materials.

Neurodegenerative diseases were identified by specialists using artificial intelligence.

Nanoparticles were harnessed by researchers in order to beat cancer.

The essential stage every battery needs to undergo, in the manufacturing process, is battery formation. Formation cycling has great impact on battery lifetime, quality and cost, but is currently the bottleneck in the production process.

Specialists work on a system for automated detection of the angle between a trailer and its tow vehicle, utilizing video from an on-board rearward facing camera. The system must be robust and operate accurately under a variety of weather and lighting conditions, and must function on a mobile processor typically found in modern vehicles.

Researchers are working on innovative methods for excluding fish species, found in freshwater rivers and estuaries in the United States, from water diversions and intakes. While effective fish exclusion for some fish species and life history stages can be achieved, improvements are needed to increase effectiveness and decrease the costs associated with fish exclusion devices. Solutions can be applied to river and canal diversions, unscreened diversion pipes, or intakes at dams

Engineers are looking for inexpensive methods that can significantly reduce or eliminate the smell perception of the odor in the cartonboard, while being applicable to a company's production line of food.

Accurate and reliable streamflow data are critical to water resources planning, management, and research. Despite the importance of streamflow data, the existing network of continuous streamflow monitoring stations (also referred to as stream gages) in the United States has declined over the past several decades. The primary driver of this decline is the cost of installing, operating, and maintaining stream gages. The engineers are seeking new and innovative methods to significantly reduce the cost of continuous streamflow monitoring compared to current methods.

Designers are working for ways to improve the comfort of an airless camping mattress. They look for designs and new materials for the internal structural components of the mattress.

Researchers are working on technologies for insect-size robots, able to perform complex jobs, like disaster relief, or inspecting hazardous environments that are inaccessible to larger robots.

In the future, wireless networks will be tasked with supporting self-driving cars, tele-health, etc. 5G is the new standard that will enable billions of IoT devices, and the networks that connect them. Smart cities are using technologies, such as 802.11ax/ay Wi-Fi, and the promise of 5G, to more efficiently manage urban environments and improve quality of life.

Engineers need the technology used in the 802.11ax amendment to the 802.11 standard, and the receiver and transmitter test requirements. IEEE 802.11ax, also known as High Efficiency Wireless (HEW), provides mechanisms to more efficiently utilize the unlicensed spectrum bands (2.4 GHz and 5 GHz), and improve user experience.

The periodic table is 150 years old in the middle of March.

Quantum computers are offering hope for solving problems that are beyond the capability of any possible conventional information processor. Individual atoms are the highest quality components for a scalable quantum computer, with unmatched coherence properties and reconfigurable circuits that are connected with laser beams. The future of this field includes the critical role lasers and optics will play.

π (Pi) Day is celebrated on March 14th around the world. Pi (Greek letter "π") is the symbol used in mathematics to represent a constant — the ratio of the circumference of a circle to its diameter — which is approximately 3.14159. π has been calculated to over one trillion digits beyond its decimal point. As an irrational and transcendental number, it will continue infinitely without repetition or pattern. Practically, only a handful of digits are needed for typical calculations. π and mathematics are permanently used in all disciplines, and they are a sine qua non requirement for doing research and innovation.

The increased demand, and the pressure for improving battery performance, have intensified the need for mathematical modeling. Modeling and simulations allow for the analysis of an almost unlimited number of design parameters and operating conditions, at a relatively small cost. Experimental tests are used to provide the necessary validation of the models.

Mathematics and AI are heavily used in cognitive modeling.

General news and issues

Report: Retired statistics professor Dr. Caleb Rossiter, with the majority of people, are very skeptic about the global warming political alarmists, with their intimidating letters, based on fake news. The climate changes up and down for over 4 billions of years.

10 March 2019. Reports: Again, billions of people are unhappy because they are forced to change their clocks, without any valid explanations. For many years, the people ask the governments to stop this unhealthy, superfluous and abusive change of time, which only please some bureaucrats.

Old aphorisms say silence is golden, but for some is not so easy. Also, being a good listener is as important a skill as being a good communicator, and intentional silence is a learned skill.

Reports: Amazon has received the last approval it was seeking for an incentive plan that helped attract the retailer to Northern Virginia. The five-member Arlington County Board on Saturday unanimously approved $23 M in incentives for Amazon to construct its HQ2 in Crystal City and agreed to spend an estimated $28 M on infrastructure improvements and open space around the buildings. Amazon has also been offered a subsidy package of up to $750 M over 15 years by the Virginia General Assembly.

20 March 2019. Reports: Jeff Bezos is hosting his annual Mars Conference this week in Palm Springs, California. The closed-door showcase displays the latest from the fields of machine learning, automation, robotics and space - hence the name, MARS. It's an annual reminder of Bezos' passion for cutting-edge technology, and how the four fields will impact the future as the Amazon founder races toward commercial space travel with Blue Origin.

Raytheon CEO Thomas Kennedy is the top executive of a $27 B company, with 67,000 employees. Regarding cybersecurity, he needs to ensure the defense contractor is at the top.

The leadership of Jack Welch at General Electric was focused on the people.

Sir Francis Galton, FRS, (16 February 1822 – 17 January 1911, aged 88.9), was an English statistician, polymath, anthropologist, tropical explorer, geographer, inventor, and meteorologist. Galton wrote over 340 papers and books. He also created the statistical concept of correlation and widely promoted regression toward the mean. He was the first to apply statistical methods to the study of human differences and inheritance of intelligence, and introduced the use of questionnaires and surveys for collecting data on human communities, which he needed for genealogical and biographical works and for his anthropometric studies. As an investigator of the human mind, he founded psychometrics (the science of measuring mental faculties) and differential psychology. He devised a method for classifying fingerprints that proved useful in forensic science. As the initiator of scientific meteorology, he devised the first weather map, proposed a theory of anticyclones, and was the first to establish a complete record of short-term climatic phenomena on a European scale. He also invented the Galton Whistle for testing differential hearing ability. He was Charles Darwin's half-cousin.

Because of the competitive pressure from Amazon.com, UPS is looking to move into the growing healthcare logistics market, with a test for a home vaccination service. In the trial, it would ship vaccines from its healthcare complex to a franchised store, where a licensed nurse would carry it the "last mile" to administer it in-house. Merck has said it's talking with UPS about the project. Outsourced healthcare logistics is an $85 B market, expected to grow to $105 B by 2021.

It will be difficult to challenge Richard Branson-backed OneWeb and Elon Musk's SpaceX. A group of private equity firms and pension funds have agreed to buy Inmarsat for $3.4 B, launching the U.K.-based satellite operator's shares up 8.4% in London. The bidders are Apax Partners, Warburg Pincus, Canada Pension Plan Investment Board, and Ontario Teachers' Pension Plan Board.

Volkswagen has agreed on a strategic partnership with Amazon to create a kind of "industry cloud," for which details will soon be announced, Germany's *Sueddeutsche* reports. The deal would likely help boost productivity of Volkswagen factories, which currently work with completely different software systems. Thousands of suppliers also connect to the plants to receive orders, but even these systems are currently not uniform.

Price cuts coming to Whole Foods at the beginning of April, as Amazon extends control on chain.

Walmart is closing at least 11 U.S. stores.

The World Health Day will be on Sunday, 7 April 2019.

Machine learning, AI and other exponentially growing technologies (all based on mathematics) are transforming businesses, the political economy, and our society on this planet.

Humor

About 1,500 years ago, in a small school near Rome, the teacher of religion asks a little boy:
- Who are the Twelve Apostles?
    The little boy promptly responds:
- The Twelve Apostles are Three: Peter and Andrew.

Italy, Rome (founded in 753 BC), Forum Caesaris (finished in 46 BC, by Julius Caesar (100 BC – 44 BC), 160 m by 75 m, with Temple of Venus Genetrix (left)), Chiesa dei Santi Luca e Martina (center right, founded in 625, rebuilt in 1669).

Universe Axioms
Formulated by Michael M. Dediu

The following axioms are not independent of each other. They express in different ways the same concept of infinity.

Axiom 1. Pointing a theoretical laser from Earth, in any direction, at any time, after a finite amount of time the laser beam will touch an astronomic body.

Axiom 2. In any direction in space starting from Earth, at any time, there is an astronomic body from which the Earth can be theoretically seen.

Axiom 3. Infinity of space: Any straight line passing through the Earth's center intersects an infinite number of astronomic bodies.

Axiom 4. Infinity of time: Representing the time on a line, with the origin at the beginning of the year 1, the time goes to infinite in both positive and negative directions.

Axiom 5. Infinity of life: Because of the infinity of space and time, it is normal to consider that the life exists at any time, in an infinite number of places. Therefore right now, when you are reading this book, there is life outside the Earth, in an infinite number of places, but we do not know yet how to contact them.

Axiom 6. The Earth rotates itself around its polar axis, the Moon and many artificial satellites rotate around the Earth, in the Solar System all the planets and many other objects rotate around the Sun, the Solar System itself rotates around the center of the Milky Way galaxy, the Milky Way galaxy and all the billions of galaxies in our Universe (denoted U_1) rotate around the center of our Universe U_1, our Universe U_1, together with billions of other similar Universes, are inside a bigger Universe U_2 and rotate around the center of U_2, then U_2 and many others like it are inside a bigger U_3 and rotate around the center of U_3, and so on. Therefore, in general, the Universe U_n together with many similar Universes are inside the bigger Universe U_{n+1} and rotate around the center of U_{n+1}, for any n natural number, which goes to infinity. This can be written in the formula:

$$U_1 \subset U_2 \subset U_3 \subset \ldots \subset U_n \subset U_{n+1} \subset \ldots, \text{ n natural number.}$$

UK, Oxford, Oriel College (1326, in the east range of First quadrangle, the ornate portico in the center, with the inscription Regnante Carolo).

Time Axioms

Formulated by Michael M. Dediu

Axiom 1. Time is the most important force in the Univers.

Axiom 2. Everything is a function of time.

Axiom 3. Time exists in absolutely everything.

Axiom 4. Time creates and distroys everything.

Axiom 5. Time is invisible, inodor, insipid, unpalpabil, unaudible, but exists evrywhere.

Axiom 6. There are infinitezimal time particles, without mass, which are present everywhere, and which actually continuously transform everything.

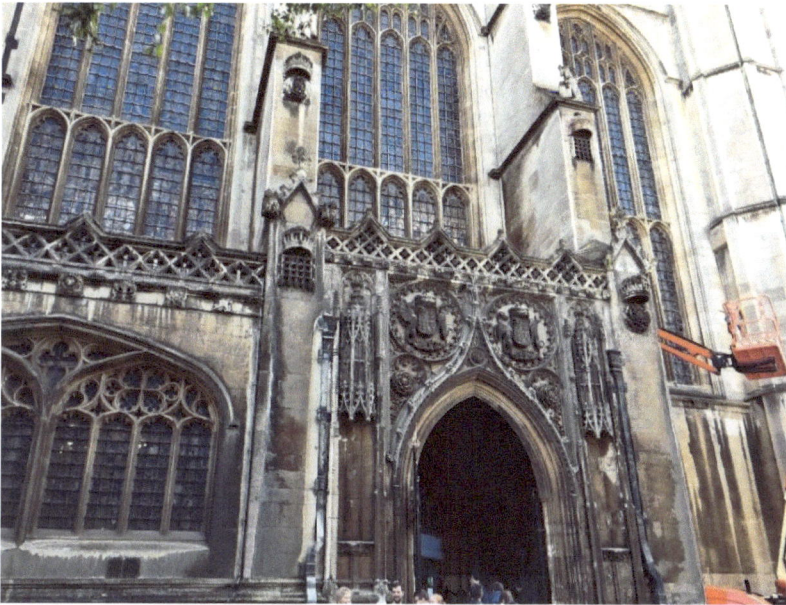

UK, Cambridge, From Trinity Lane looking south to the west part of the northern façade and entrance of King's College Chapel (1446).

Bibliography

"The Histories" by Polybius
"Discours de la Méthode" by René Descartes
"Meditationes de prima philosophia" by René Descartes
"Philosophiae Naturalis Principia Mathematica" by Isaac Newton
Chinese encyclopedia Gujin Tushu Jicheng (Imperial Encyclopedia)
"Encyclopédie" by Jean-Baptiste le Rond d'Alembert and Denis Diderot
"Encyclopaedia Britannica" by over 4,400 contributors
"Encyclopedia Americana" by Francis Lieber

Michael M. Dediu is also the author of these books (which can be found on Amazon.com, and www.derc.com):

1. Aphorisms and quotations – with examples and explanations
2. Axioms, aphorisms and quotations – with examples and explanations
3. 100 Great Personalities and their Quotations
4. Professor Petre P. Teodorescu – A Great Mathematician and Engineer
5. Professor Ioan Goia – A Dedicated Engineering Professor
6. Venice (Venezia) – a new perspective. A short presentation with photographs
7. La Serenissima (Venice) - a new photographic perspective. A short presentation with many photos
8. Grand Canal – Venice. A new photographic viewpoint. A short presentation with many photos
9. Piazza San Marco – Venice. A different photographic view. A short presentation with many photos
10. Roma (Rome) - La Città Eterna. A new photographic view. A short presentation with many photos
11. Why is Rome so Fascinating? A short presentation with many photos
12. Rome, Boston and Helsinki. A short photographic presentation
13. Rome and Tokyo – two captivating cities. A short photographic presentation
14. Beautiful Places on Earth – A new photographic presentation

15. From Niagara Falls to Mount Fuji via Rome - A novel photographic presentation

16. From the USA and Canada to Italy and Japan - A fresh photographic presentation

17. Paris – Why So Many Call This City Mon Amour - A lovely photographic presentation

18. The City of Light – Paris (La Ville-Lumière) - A kaleidoscopic photographic presentation

19. Paris (Lutetia Parisiorum) – the romance capital of the world - A kaleidoscopic photographic view

20. Paris and Tokyo – a joyful photographic presentation. With a preamble about the Universe

21. From USA to Japan via Canada – A cheerful photographic documentary

22. 200 Wonderful Places, In The Last 50 Years – A personal photographic documentary

23. Must see places in USA and Japan - A kaleidoscopic photographic documentary

24. Grandeurs of the World - A kaleidoscopic photographic documentary

25. Corneliu Leu – writer on the same wavelength as Mark Twain. An American viewpoint

26. From Berkeley to Pompeii via Rome – A kaleidoscopic photographic documentary

27. From America to Europe via Japan - A kaleidoscopic photographic documentary

28. Discover America and Japan - A photographic documentary

29. J. R. Lucas – philosopher on a creative parallel with Plato, An American viewpoint

30. From America to Switzerland via France - A photographic documentary

31. From Bretton Woods to New York via Cape Cod - A photographic documentary

32. Splendid Places on the Atlantic Coast of the U. S. A. - A photographic documentary

33. Fourteen nice Cities on three Continents - A photographic documentary

34. 17 Picturesque Cities on the World Map - A photographic documentary

35. Unforgettable Places from Four Continents, including Trump buildings - A photographic documentary

36. Dediu Newsletter, Volume 1, Number 1, 6 December 2016 – Monthly news, review, comments and suggestions for a better and wiser world

37. Dediu Newsletter, Volume 1, Number 2, 6 January 2017 (available also at www.derc.com).

38. Dediu Newsletter, Volume 1, Number 3, 6 February 2017 (available at www.derc.com).

39. London and Greenwich, - A photographic documentary

40. Dediu Newsletter, Volume 1, Number 4, 6 March 2017 (available also at www.derc.com).

41. Dediu Newsletter, Volume 1, Number 5, 6 April 2017 (available also at www.derc.com).

42. Dediu Newsletter, Volume 1, Number 6, 6 May 2017 (available also at www.derc.com).

43. Dediu Newsletter, Volume 1, Number 7, 6 June 2017 (available also at www.derc.com).

44. London, Oxford and Cambridge, A photographic documentary

45. Dediu Newsletter, Volume 1, Number 8, 6 July 2017 (available also at www.derc.com).

46. Dediu Newsletter, Volume 1, Number 9, 6 August 2017 (available also at www.derc.com).

47. Dediu Newsletter, Volume 1, Number 10, 6 September 2017 (available also at www.derc.com).

48. Three Great Professors: President Woodrow Wilson, Historian German Arciniegas, and Mathematician Gheorghe Vranceanu – A chronological and photographic documentary

49. Dediu Newsletter, Volume 1, Number 11, 6 October 2017 (available also at www.derc.com).

50. Dediu Newsletter, Volume 1, Number 12, 6 November 2017 (available also at www.derc.com).

51. Dediu Newsletter, Volume 2, Number 1 (13), 6 December 2017 (available also at www.derc.com).

52. Two Great Leaders: Augustus and George Washington - A chronological and photographic documentary

53. Dediu Newsletter, Volume 2, Number 2 (14), 6 January 2018 (available also at www.derc.com).

54. Newton, Benjamin Franklin, and Gauss, A chronological and photographic documentary
55. Dediu Newsletter, Volume 2, Number 3 (15), 6 February 2018 (available also at www.derc.com).
56. 2017: World Top Events, But Many Little Known, A chronological and photographic documentary
57. Dediu Newsletter, Volume 2, Number 4 (16), 6 March 2018 (available also at www.derc.com).
58. Vergilius, Horatius, Ovidius, and Shakespeare - A chronological and photographic documentary.
59. Dediu Newsletter, Volume 2, Number 5 (17), 6 April 2018 (available also at www.derc.com).
60. Dediu Newsletter, Volume 2, Number 6 (18), 6 May 2018 (available also at www.derc.com).
61. Vivaldi, Bach, Mozart, and Verdi - A chronological and photographic documentary.
62. Dediu Newsletter, Volume 2, Number 7 (19), 6 June 2018 (available also at www.derc.com).
63. Dediu Newsletter, Volume 2, Number 8 (20), 6 July 2018 (available also at www.derc.com).
64. Dediu Newsletter, Volume 2, Number 9 (21), 6 August 2018 (available also at www.derc.com).
65. World History, a new perspective - A chronological and photographic documentary.
66. World Humor History with over 100 Jokes, a new perspective - A chronological and photographic documentary
67. Dediu Newsletter, Volume 2, Number 10 (22), 6 September 2018 (available also at www.derc.com).
68. Dediu Newsletter, Volume 2, Number 11 (23), 6 October 2018 (available also at www.derc.com).
69. Dediu Newsletter, Volume 2, Number 12 (24), 6 November 2018
70. Da Vinci, Michelangelo, Rembrandt, Rodin - A chronological and photographic documentary
71. Dediu Newsletter, Volume 3, Number 1 (25), 6 December 2018
72. Dediu Newsletter, Volume 3, Number 2 (26), 6 January 2019
73. From Euclid to Edison – revelries in the past 75 years - A chronological and photographic documentary

74. – Socrates to Churchill Aphorisms celebrated after 1960 - A chronological and photographic documentary
75. - Dediu Newsletter, Volume 3, Number 3 (27), 6 February 2019
76. – Hippocrates to Fleming: Medicine History celebrated after 1943 - A chronological and photographic documentary
77. - Dediu Newsletter, Volume 3, Number 4 (28), 6 March 2019

USA, Boston, 3 Dec 2009, from Avenue Louis Pasteur (1822-1895, French microbiologist), Boston Public Latin School (1635, Schola Latina Bostoniensis, the oldest and the first public exam school in the U.S.).

Mathematical research papers published in international mathematical journals

1. Dediu, M. On the lens spaces. *Rev. Roumaine Math. Pures Appl.* **14** (1969) 623-627.

2. Dediu, M. Sur quelques propriétés des espaces lenticulaires. (French) *Rev. Roumaine Math. Pures Appl.* **17** (1972), 871-874.

3. Vranceanu, G; Dediu, M. Tangent vector fields in projective spaces V_3 and in the lens spaces $L^3(3)$. (Romanian) Stud. Cerc. Mat. **24** (1972), 1585-1600.

4. Dediu, M. Tangent vector fields on lens spaces of dimension three (Italian) *Atti Accad. Naz. Lincei Rend. Cl. Sci. Fis. Mat. Natur.* **54** (1974), no. 2, 329-334 (1977

5. Dediu, M. Campi di vettori tangenti sullo spazio lenticolare $L^7(3)$. (Italian) *Atti Accad. Naz. Lincei Rend. Cl. Sci. Fis. Mat. Natur. (8)* **58** (1975), no. 1, 14-17.

6. Dediu, M. Tre campi di vettori tangenti indepedenti sugli spazi lenticolari di dimensione $4n+3$. (Italian) *Atti Accad. Naz. Lincei Rend. Cl. Sci. Fis. Mat. Natur. (8)* **58** (1975), no. 2, 174-178.

7. Dediu, M. Sopra la metrica Vranceanu generalizzata (Italian) *Atti Accad. Naz. Lincei Rend. Cl. Sci. Fis. Mat. Natur. (8)* **58** (1975), no.3, 354-359).

8. Dediu, M. Sopra la metrica Vranceanu generalizzata (Italian) *Atti Accad. Naz. Lincei Rend. Cl. Sci. Fis. Mat. Natur. (8)* **58** (1975), no.3, 354-359).

9. Dediu, S.; Dediu, M. Sopra gli spazi proiettivi. *Rend. Sem. Fac. Sci. Univ. Cagliari* **46** (1976), suppl., 149-152.

10. Dediu, M.; Caddeo, Renzo; Dediu Sofia Alcune proprietà di una superficie immersa in uno spazio di Hilbert. (Italian) *Rend. Ist. Mat. Univ. Trieste* **8** (1976), no. 2, 147-161 (1977)

11. Dediu, S.; Dediu, M.; Caddeo, R. Alcune proprietà della metrica di Vranceanu generalizzata. (Italian) *Rend Sem. Fac. Sci. Univ Cagliari* **46** (1976), suppl., 153-161.

12. Dediu, Sofia; Dediu, M.; Caddeo, Renzo The Vrănceanu metric in local coordinates. (Italian) *Atti Accad. Sci. Lett. Arti Palermo Parte I (4)* **37** (1977/78). 331-339 (1980)

13. Dediu, M.; Caddeo, Renzo; Dediu, Sofia The extension of an *E*-premanifold to an *E*-manifold. (Italian) *Rend. Circ. Mat. Palermo (2)* **27** (1978), no. 3, 353-358.

Japan: the northern side of Kawaguchiko (Lake Kawaguchi, 6 km^2, 830 m elevation), with a splendid statue (left), 17 km north of Mt. Fuji (3,776 m, 1707 last eruption), 100 km south-west of Tokyo.

Michael M. Dediu is the editor of these books (also on Amazon.com, and www.derc.com):

1. Sophia Dediu: The life and its torrents – Ana. In Europe around 1920
2. Proceedings of the 4th International Conference "Advanced Composite Materials Engineering" COMAT 2012
3. Adolf Shvedchikov: I am an eternal child of spring – poems in English, Italian, French, German, Spanish and Russian
4. Adolf Shvedchikov: Life's Enigma – poems in English, Italian and Russian
5. Adolf Shvedchikov: Everyone wants to be HAPPY – poems in English, Spanish and Russian
6. Adolf Shvedchikov: My Life, My Love – poems in English, Italian and Russian
7. Adolf Shvedchikov: I am the gardener of love – poems in English and Russian
8. Adolf Shvedchikov: Amaretta di Saronno – poems in English and Russian
9. Adolf Shvedchikov: A Russian Rediscovers America
10. Adolf Shvedchikov: Parade of Life - poems in English and Russian
11. Adolf Shvedchikov: Overcoming Sorrow - poems in English and Russian
12. Sophia Dediu: Sophia meets Japan
13. Corneliu Leu: Roosevelt, Churchill, Stalin and Hitler: Their surprising role in Eastern Europe in 1944
14. Proceedings of the 5th International Conference "Computational Mechanics and Virtual Engineering" COMEC 2013
15. Georgeta Simion – Potanga: Beyond Imagination: A Thought-provoking novel inspired from mid-20th century events
16. Ana Dediu: The poetry of my life in Europe and The USA
17. Ana Dediu: The Four Graces
18. Proceedings of the 5th International Conference "Advanced Composite Materials Engineering" COMAT 2014
19. Sophia Dediu: Chocolate Cook Book: Is there such a thing as too much chocolate?

20. Sorin Vlase: Mechanical Identifiability in Automotive Engineering

21. Gabriel Dima: The Evolution of the Aerostructures – Concept and Technologies

22. Proceedings of the 6th International Conference "Computational Mechanics and Virtual Engineering" COMEC 2015

23. Sophia Dediu: Cook Book 1 A-B-C Common sense cooking

24. Sophia Dediu: Dim Sum Spring Festival

25. Ana Dediu and Sophia Dediu: Europe in 1985: A chronological and photographic documentary

26. Stefan Staretu: Europe: Serbian Despotate of Srem and the Romanian Area – Between the 14th and the 16th Centuries

Washington, D.C. (1790) in 2007, National Gallery of Art (1937, in the National Mall).